HISTORICAL AGES

THE PALEO-INDIAN PERIOD

BY EMMA KAISER

CONTENT CONSULTANT
Arthur Anderson, PhD
Associate Teaching Professor, Archaeology
School of Social and Behavioral Sciences
University of New England

Core Library

An Imprint of Abdo Publishing
abdobooks.com

Cover image: During the Paleo-Indian Period, people lived as hunter-gatherers. They hunted animals and gathered plants to eat.

abdobooks.com

Published by Abdo Publishing, a division of ABDO, PO Box 398166, Minneapolis, Minnesota 55439.

Printed in the United States of America, North Mankato, Minnesota.
102024
012025

Cover Photo: North Wind Picture Archives/Alamy
Interior Photos: John Hibma/Alamy, 4–5; George Ostertag/Alamy, 7; Ian Dagnall/Alamy, 9; Chase Studio/Science Source, 12, 19, 45; Natural History Library/Alamy, 14–15; Mikkel Juul Jensen/Science Source, 16; Jim Lane/Education Images/Universal Images Group/Getty Images, 22–23; Tom McHugh/Science Source, 25; Mauricio Anton/Science Source, 26–27; Folsom Village, 29; Logan Bush/Shutterstock Images, 30; Werner Forman/Universal Images Group/Getty Images, 32–33; Jeff Whyte/Shutterstock Images, 35, 43; Witold Skrypczak/Alamy, 37; Red Line Editorial, 39; Fred Bunch/National Park Service, 40

Editor: Laura Stickney
Series Designer: Ryan Gale

Library of Congress Control Number: 2024938492

Publisher's Cataloging-in-Publication Data

Names: Kaiser, Emma, author.
Title: The Paleo-Indian period / by Emma Kaiser
Description: Minneapolis, Minnesota: ABDO Publishing, 2025 | Series: Historical ages | Includes online resources and index.
Identifiers: ISBN 9781098295653 (lib. bdg.) | ISBN 9798384916659 (ebook)
Subjects: LCSH: History, Ancient--Juvenile literature. | Paleolithic period--Juvenile literature. | Paleo-Indians--Juvenile literature. | Nomads--Juvenile literature. | Hunting and gathering societies--Juvenile literature. | History--Juvenile literature. | Archaeology--Juvenile literature. | Anthropology, Prehistoric--Juvenile literature.
Classification: DDC 930.12--dc23

CONTENTS

CHAPTER ONE

AN IMPORTANT DISCOVERY

In 2019, a bridge was scheduled to be built over the Farmington River in Avon, Connecticut. State law required that an archaeological investigation take place before construction started. Archaeologists ran tests on the soil in the area. They had tested the soil in 2014 as well. The tests suggested that something important might be buried in the soil at the construction site. The archaeologists decided to fully investigate the site. When they started digging, they made a huge discovery.

The Brian D. Jones Paleoindian Site was discovered about five to seven feet (1.5–2.1 m) below the ground near the banks of Farmington River, *pictured*.

It was evidence of ancient peoples who had once lived at the site.

The excavation in Avon took three months. When archaeologists dug a trench about three feet (0.9 m) deep, they found an ancient artifact. When they dug the next hole, they found 87 more items. By the time the excavation was finished, the team of archaeologists had found 15,000 stone artifacts. These included spearpoints and tools that were more than 12,000 years old. Several similar objects had been found in the state before the excavation took place. The site in Avon was later called the Brian D. Jones Paleoindian Site. It was named after one of the archaeologists who first suspected that the site might be important.

The artifacts discovered at the Brian D. Jones site came from a historical period known as the Paleo-Indian Period. The artifacts found at the site belonged to some of the very first people to live in New England, the northeastern region of the United States. That made the site one of the oldest archaeological sites

Today, people can't see much at the Brian D. Jones site because a bridge was built there after the excavation. But people can explore land near the site at Fisher Meadows Recreation Area.

in New England. Discoveries such as those from the Brian D. Jones site help archaeologists learn more about what life was like for early North Americans thousands of years ago.

MASTODONS

Mastodons were large mammals that looked similar to elephants. They had long tusks and thick reddish-brown fur. They first appeared about 23 million years ago and went extinct about 10,000 to 13,000 years ago. They lived all around the world. Many mastodon remains have been discovered and studied. Human hunting may have been one of the reasons the mastodon went extinct.

LIFE IN THE PALEO-INDIAN PERIOD

About 25,000 to 16,000 years ago, Connecticut was covered in ice more than two miles (3 km) thick. As time passed, the ice melted and glaciers started to recede. This meant more living things could survive in the region. Large animals such as mastodons, caribou, and giant beavers moved into the area. People may have followed these animals there to hunt them. While studying tools uncovered at the Brian D. Jones site, scientists found traces of blood that likely came from a mastodon. This suggests that early Paleo-Indian peoples hunted large animals in the region.

Archaeologists have discovered mastodon bones throughout North America. People can see a mastodon skeleton at the La Brea Tar Pits and Museum in Los Angeles, California.

Paleo-Indian artifacts help archaeologists determine what kind of diet people may have had during the period. Paleo-Indian peoples hunted animals and ate local plants. Grinding stones found at the Brian D. Jones site show evidence that they were used for grinding plant roots. This gives experts clues about what people ate and what kind of climate Connecticut had during the period. For a long time, archaeologists believed the region had been covered in evergreen trees. But the Brian D. Jones discovery suggested that trees with broad leaves grew in the area too.

RADIOCARBON DATING

Radiocarbon dating, or carbon dating, is a method by which scientists determine the age of artifacts or remains. The process can usually reliably determine the age of artifacts up to 57,300 years old. It works by measuring the presence of the element carbon 14 in plants and animals. All living things absorb carbon 14 into their tissues. When a living thing dies, the carbon 14 decays, or breaks down, over time. Scientists calculate the age of an artifact by counting how many carbon 14 atoms remain in it compared with other elements.

Other artifacts discovered at the site included spearpoints and scraping tools. Tools made of wood or bone would have broken down over time. But these stone tools lasted thousands of years.

No human remains were found at the Brian D. Jones site. But archaeologists found evidence of human-made shelters. One discovery was a hearth with charcoal in it. Scientists tested the charcoal and discovered that it was 12,500 years old. This suggested that people likely had a settlement at the site. It was a place where people lived, worked, and prepared food.

STUDYING THE PALEO-INDIAN PERIOD

The term *Paleo-Indian* comes from the Latin word *palaeo*, meaning "old or ancient." The dates of the Paleo-Indian Period's beginning and end vary. This is because Paleo-Indian peoples traveled to and settled in different parts of North and South America at different times. Some experts say that the Paleo-Indian Period lasted from 16,000 BCE to 7500 BCE. People who lived during the period were hunter-gatherers. They survived by eating food they could gather or hunt. They likely lived in small groups of 20 to 60 people. They moved around to find food.

The Paleo-Indian Period is divided into three different stages. These are the Early, Middle, and Late Paleo-Indian Periods. It's difficult to know much about the Paleo-Indian Period because it happened

During the Paleo-Indian Period, people used traps and tools such as spears to hunt large animals, including mammoths.

so long ago. Few artifacts from the period have survived long enough for archaeologists to find them. But over time, Paleo-Indian excavations across the continent have taught archaeologists more about the first people who lived in North and South America.

STRAIGHT TO THE

SOURCE

David Leslie is an archaeologist who worked at the Brian D. Jones site in Connecticut. In an interview with a reporter from *Connecticut Magazine*, Leslie said:

> *This isn't the story of the first people to arrive in America, but a story of when people started to populate this region as the environment was changing. It's a breathtaking view into what life was like. . . . At this site, in the first month and a half of excavating, we found new and exciting discoveries on a daily basis. . . . There is evidence for people accessing a variety of wetland resources. . . . There are a number of different food resources from plants that aren't expected but were not known from this time period before now. . . . The collection of all these things at one site is important.*

Source: Janet Reynolds. "Archeological Digs in CT Shed Light on Humans Who Lived over 10,000 Years Ago." *CT Insider*, 11 Jan. 2022, ctinsider.com. Accessed 16 Apr. 2024.

BACK IT UP

The author of this passage is using evidence to support a point. Write a paragraph describing the point the author is making. Then write down two or three pieces of evidence the author uses to make the point.

CHAPTER TWO

EARLY PALEO-INDIAN PERIOD

Many archaeologists believe humans migrated to North and South America by crossing a large piece of land. This piece of land acted as a bridge. The land bridge connected modern-day Siberia, an area in Asia located northeast of Russia, to modern-day Alaska.

This land bridge is known as the Bering Land Bridge. The small landmass was only 55 miles (89 km) long but up to 1,000 miles (1,600 km) wide. It connected

The Bering Land Bridge National Preserve in Alaska protects the remains of the Bering Land Bridge. Today, the Bering Strait flows where the bridge used to be.

EARLY HUMAN MIGRATION

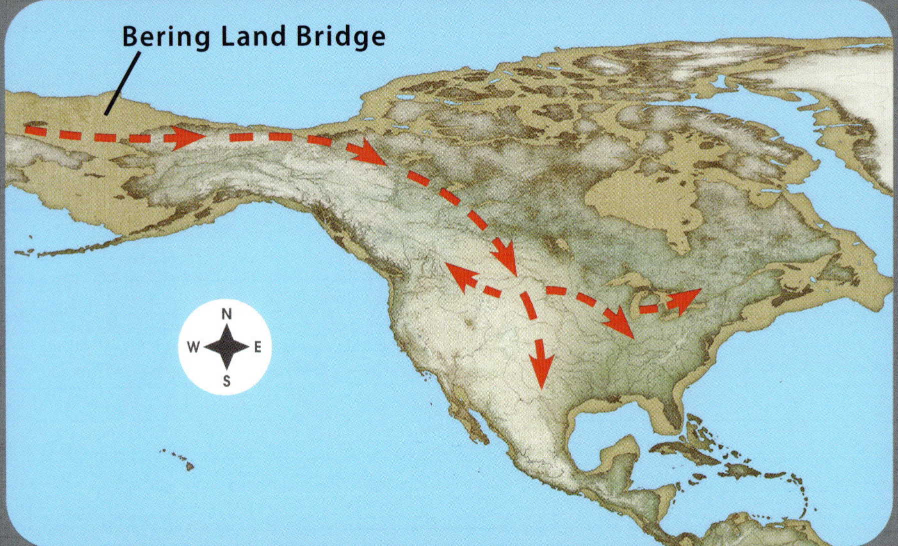

This map shows a route that early humans may have taken across the Bering Land Bridge into North America. Why do you think people took this route? How does the map help you better understand the text?

North America and Asia. The Bering Land Bridge still exists, but it is now underwater. People can no longer cross it on foot or study what people may have left behind on it. Some archaeologists believe people began migrating across the Bering Land Bridge as early as 40,000 to 30,000 years ago.

People likely arrived on foot and then migrated throughout the continent over several thousand years.

Some people appear to have traveled south from Alaska by foot. Others likely traveled by boat down North America's Pacific coast. This may have been how people reached South America.

It is difficult to know how and when humans first migrated to parts of North and South America. Archaeologists study artifacts such as stone tools to try to determine how old they are and when they were used. But few artifacts from the period have survived long enough to be studied. It's also difficult to determine exactly how old an

CHANGING SEA LEVELS

The Bering Land Bridge existed because thousands of years ago, Earth's oceans were lower than they are today. During the last Ice Age (120,000–11,500 years ago), much of Earth's water was frozen in glaciers. Sea levels may have been as much as 400 feet (120 m) lower than they are today. Due to these low sea levels, a cold tundra with grassy areas formed. This allowed animals and humans to cross from Asia into North America.

object is. As archaeologists continue to learn more, some have come to believe humans have occupied the Americas much longer than previously thought. Some archaeologists have discovered evidence that suggests humans reached the Americas around 12,000 years ago. Others believe it could have been more than 25,000 years ago. Archaeologists are still learning new things about the first people in the Americas. They call this period the Early Paleo-Indian Period.

THE CLOVIS CULTURE

One of the first groups to enter modern-day Canada and the United States was the Clovis Culture. This group is named after an archaeological site discovered near Clovis, New Mexico. The Clovis Culture is known for the style of stone spearheads they made. These spearpoints are called Clovis points. They narrow to a point at the end. The points were made by chipping off flakes of stone with a rounded stone called a hammerstone. Clovis points also have a groove called a flute flaked

The Clovis people used tools such as stone points, scrapers, and hammerstones. Scrapers may have been used to scrape animal skins so they could be used for clothing.

into their bases and sides. This helped people attach the Clovis points to wooden shafts.

Clovis people used these spears to hunt large animals. They hunted mammoths, giant sloths, horses, saber-toothed tigers, giant beavers, and bison. At sites

CLOVIS FIRST?

For a long time, archaeologists believed the Clovis people were the first to inhabit North America. But more recent discoveries have challenged that theory. One is the Monte Verde site in Chile, located near the southern tip of South America. Archaeologists have discovered rare artifacts at the site, including grass rope, animal hides, and the foundation of a building. Through carbon dating, some artifacts discovered at Monte Verde in 2013 were found to be between 14,500 and 19,000 years old. The people who left behind these artifacts were not Clovis people. The discoveries at Monte Verde suggest that people were in South America long before the Clovis people were.

such as the Naco Mammoth Kill Site in Arizona, archaeologists have discovered Clovis points alongside the bones of these types of animals. This evidence suggests that the animals were killed by Clovis hunters.

DNA from early human remains found in Montana suggests that Clovis people originally came from Asia. Over time, they migrated south through Canada and into modern-day Montana. There, archaeologists have discovered Clovis tools that are between 12,725 and 12,900 years old. The Clovis people followed large animals across the continent. They traveled to places where they could hunt. Many other North American peoples and cultures descended from the Clovis people.

FURTHER EVIDENCE

Chapter Two talks about different ways that people may have migrated to North and South America. What is the main point of this chapter? What key evidence supports this point? Go to the article about the Paleo-Indian Period at the website below. Find a quote from the website that supports the chapter's main point.

PALEO INDIANS

abdocorelibrary.com/paleo-indian-period

CHAPTER THREE

MIDDLE PALEO-INDIAN PERIOD

In the Middle Paleo-Indian Period, the land was different than it had been during the Early Paleo-Indian Period. During this time, many animals went extinct. The planet warmed up, causing glaciers to melt. As a result, sea levels rose. This changed the landscape and terrain. These changes, possibly along with human hunting, led to the extinction of animals such as horses, camels, and mammoths in the Americas. The changing climate also meant that humans had to hunt

Ice Age animal remains have been found at Big Bone Lick State Historic Site in Kentucky. Paleo-Indian people may have hunted mammoths, ground sloths, and bison there.

and feed themselves differently. People likely relied on different animals and plants than before.

PALEO-INDIAN HUNTERS

When people first arrived in the Americas, the animals living there weren't used to humans. They didn't know how to defend themselves against human hunters. This made animals easier targets. People would stalk an animal and then attack it with their pointed spears. Once the animal was wounded, the hunters would chase it to tire it out and then kill it. Another hunting technique was forcing herds of animals to stampede over a cliff. This resulted in many kills at once and could feed a group of people for a long time.

THE FOLSOM CULTURE

One important Middle Paleo-Indian group was the Folsom Culture. It existed between 9000 BCE and 8000 BCE. The Folsom Culture likely descended from the Clovis Culture. Folsom people lived mainly in central North America, across the Great Plains. The Great Plains region spreads across much of modern-day Montana,

Most Folsom points look similar to Clovis points but are shorter and have flutes along their entire length.

Wyoming, North Dakota, South Dakota, and other central US states.

Clovis people had mainly hunted mammoths. When mammoths went extinct, Folsom people had to change their hunting methods. Like the Clovis Culture, the Folsom Culture was known for making leaf-shaped spearpoints. But Folsom spearpoints were made mainly

Folsom people hunted an ancient species of bison called *Bison antiquus*. These bison were taller and had longer horns than modern bison.

for hunting bison, which were faster and smaller than mammoths. Like Clovis points, Folsom points were attached to throwing spears. The most distinct artifacts discovered from the Folsom Culture are spearpoints, but archaeologists have also found scraping tools and knives.

The Folsom people used bison for food. They also used parts of the animal to make clothing and tools. The people lived in small groups and followed bison herds.

They likely traveled long distances when bison herds were active. During other times of the year, the Folsom people spent time in places where there was water, stone for tools, and edible plants. They also hunted smaller animals such as sheep, deer, and rabbits.

FOLSOM DISCOVERIES

The Folsom Culture is named after an archaeological site near Folsom, New Mexico. The site was discovered by George McJunkin in 1908. McJunkin was a Black

PALEO-INDIAN PEOPLE IN THE RAINFOREST

For a long time, archaeologists thought the Amazon rainforest in South America was too damp and forested for Paleo-Indian peoples. But the discovery of a painted cave in Brazil showed that ancient people survived in tropical areas. Unlike the Folsom Culture, early people in the Amazon rainforest lived in small rock shelters. In 1996, the cave in Brazil was excavated. Archaeologists found spearpoints, tools, and plant and animal remains that were 11,000 years old. These artifacts suggested that people foraged for nuts, seeds, and tropical fruits. They hunted small animals such as fish, birds, and reptiles.

man who had been formerly enslaved in Texas. He later settled in New Mexico, where he worked as a bison hunter and ranch worker.

In 1908, a flood took place in Folsom. McJunkin was fixing a fence that had been damaged in the flood when he discovered something odd. The flood had uncovered ancient bison bones in the ground.

For years, McJunkin tried to tell people about the site,

George McJunkin discovered ancient bison bones in the Wild Horse Arroyo, located along the Dry Cimarron River in New Mexico. The area is now known as the Folsom site.

but no one was interested. Finally, others reached out to the Denver Museum of Natural History about the site. This led to a full excavation of the site in 1926. The discovery of the Folsom site, including stone tools that were found there, showed that people had been present in that part of the continent by at least

9000 BCE. There was also evidence that about 32 bison had been trapped and hunted at the site using stone spearpoints. These tools would later be known as Folsom points. Since then, thousands of Folsom points have been found at more than 1,500 archaeological sites across central North America.

EXPLORE ONLINE

Chapter Three discusses how archaeologists study artifacts to learn more about the Paleo-Indian Period. The website below explores life during the Paleo-Indian Period. As you know, every source is different. How is the information from the website similar to the information in Chapter Two? What new information did you learn from the website?

DISCOVER THE PALEO-INDIAN PEOPLE

abdocorelibrary.com/paleo-indian-period

At some US museums, visitors can see skeletons of the type of ancient bison that the Folsom people hunted.

32

CHAPTER FOUR

LATE PALEO-INDIAN PERIOD

Toward the end of the Paleo-Indian Period, people began making changes to their tools and weapons. One of the most important changes was the transition from fluted to nonfluted spearpoints. Clovis and Folsom points had arched grooves, or flutes, flaked down either side. This allowed them to be attached to spear handles. Fluted points were better for piercing through thick animal hides. Nonfluted spearpoints could be used as darts. These points were used

Archaeologists have names for different types of Paleo-Indian points. Some points are described as lanceolate, meaning they are shaped like lances.

for hunting smaller animals, such as deer.

LIVING OFF THE LAND

During the Paleo-Indian Period, people spent most of their time on the move. Archaeologists have very little evidence of what Paleo-Indian shelters looked like. But people likely dug pits or used bark, brush, or animal skins to protect themselves against the wind and cold. Paleo-Indian people relied on nature for their needs. They knew which rocks to use for blades and spearpoints. They used wood from trees to make handles for spears and tools. They also used animal skins for shoes, clothes, and blankets.

PLANO CULTURES

Some of the earliest nonfluted points in western North America are Plano points, which are named after the Plano cultures. These people lived on the plains in an area stretching from modern-day central Canada to the Gulf of Mexico. Plano people were likely descendants of the Folsom Culture. They lived in around 8000 BCE.

At that time, the continent's landscape was changing. The climate became warmer and drier.

Paleo-Indian artifacts have been found at sites such as Head-Smashed-In Buffalo Jump World Heritage Site in Alberta, Canada. Hunters killed bison by chasing them off cliffs.

This caused the land in some places to become more forested. Trees grew in places that had previously been cold and icy. This attracted different types of animals. Instead of mammoths and mastodons, there were more deer, elk, and antelope in the area.

The Clovis and Folsom peoples hunted specific animals, such as mammoths. But toward the end of the Paleo-Indian Period, people became more general hunters. They learned how to hunt many different animals, rather than just a few.

THE CODY COMPLEX

The Cody Complex was one of the largest Plano cultures that lived during the Late Paleo-Indian Period. The group is named for an archaeological site in Cody, Wyoming. Another Paleo-Indian site was discovered on a Colorado ranch in 1957. It was called the Olsen-Chubbuck Bison Kill Site. Soil had been worn away, causing bison bones to become exposed. Archaeologists discovered dozens of spearpoints and stone tools at the site, along with the remains of more than 190 bison.

By dating the bison bones, archaeologists were able to date the site to around 8200 BCE. At that time, Paleo-Indian people had forced a herd of bison to

An exhibit at the Head-Smashed-In Buffalo Jump Interpretive Center shows how Paleo-Indian people hunted bison. People continued this hunting practice after the Paleo-Indian Period.

stampede and fall over a short cliff into a gully. Once the bison were trapped in the gully, the hunters used weapons to kill any surviving bison. The meat from this kill likely totaled about 60,000 pounds (27,216 kg). It would have taken 150 to 200 people and dogs to carry and eat the meat.

PALEO-INDIAN DOGS

Many archaeologists believe that Paleo-Indian groups had dogs. Finding evidence of dog remains is very rare. Dogs would have first been domesticated from wolves in Asia. They likely followed people into North America across the Bering Land Bridge. Dogs may have helped Paleo-Indian people hunt game. They may also have carried things as people moved from place to place.

END OF THE PALEO-INDIAN PERIOD

The Paleo-Indian Period came to an end between 9600 BCE and 7500 BCE. The time after this period is known as the Archaic Period. During this time, people continued to use nonfluted

EARLY HISTORICAL STAGES

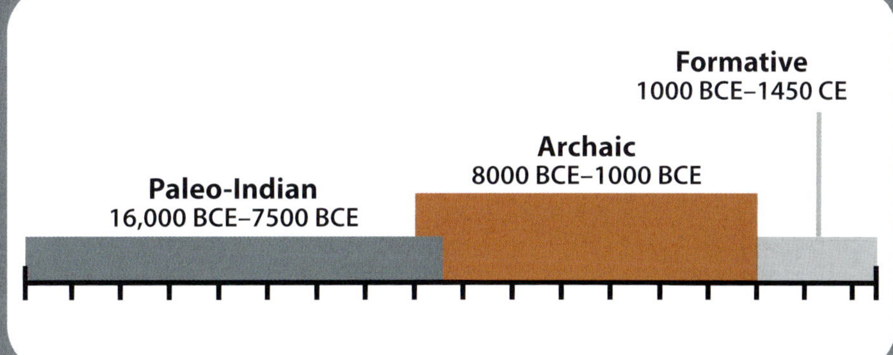

This timeline shows the dates of the Paleo-Indian Period and the Archaic Period. It also shows the Formative Period, which followed the Archaic. What do you notice about where these periods fall on the timeline? How do you think each period influenced the ones that came after it?

spearpoints. But weapons changed. One tool was called the atlatl. It was developed in the Late Paleo-Indian Period and was commonly used by Archaic peoples. The atlatl was a wooden staff with a hook made of bone or antler at the end. The hunter's spear rested on the hook. The atlatl helped hunters throw spears farther.

The climate became more stable during the Archaic Period. It became even warmer and drier than before. Different plants and animals began to inhabit the area. The people who lived during the Archaic Period traveled

At some US national parks, people can attend atlatl demonstrations. They can try using a replica of an Archaic atlatl.

less than people in the Paleo-Indian Period. They began to form settlements and stay in one place for longer amounts of time. People continued to adapt to their changing environment. But they carried with them the lifestyles and hunting methods of the very first people to live in North and South America.

STRAIGHT TO THE SOURCE

Some US national parks, such as Yellowstone National Park, include sites related to the Paleo-Indian Period. The National Park Service website says:

> *The Cody Complex is named for a [bison] kill site near Cody, Wyoming. It is believed that these Paleoindians visited [what is now Yellowstone National Park] during the summer to hunt and while they were here, they collected obsidian for tools. The Osprey Beach site is a 9,400 year old camp at nearly 7,300 feet [2.2 km] where several families spent time on Yellowstone Lake repairing and manufacturing tools. They used blocks of local sandstone to shape their wooden shafts. The large number of obsidian tools found [at] Osprey Beach is changing the view that Paleoindians did not use obsidian, which had been thought by some archaeologists to be too brittle a stone from which to make these . . . points.*

Source: "Paleoindian Period." *National Park Service*, 31 July 2015, nps.gov. Accessed 16 Apr. 2024.

WHAT'S THE BIG IDEA?

Take a close look at this passage. What is the main connection being made between Yellowstone National Park and the Cody Complex? What views about Paleo-Indian people are changing?

IMPORTANT DATES

40,000–30,000 years ago
People begin migrating from Asia to North America across the Bering Land Bridge.

16,000 BCE
The Paleo-Indian Period begins.

9000 BCE
The Folsom Culture begins.

8200 BCE
Paleo-Indian people successfully hunt and kill a herd of 190 bison at the Olsen-Chubbuck Bison Kill Site.

8000 BCE
The Plano cultures live throughout parts of North America.

9600–7500 BCE
The Paleo-Indian Period ends.

1908 CE
George McJunkin discovers artifacts from the Folsom Culture at a site in Folsom, New Mexico.

1957
The Olsen-Chubbuck Bison Kill Site is discovered on a ranch.

2019
Archaeologists uncover Paleo-Indian artifacts while excavating the Brian D. Jones site in Connecticut.

STOP AND THINK

Tell the Tale

Chapter One of this book discusses the excavation of the Brian D. Jones site in Connecticut. Imagine you are an archaeologist at an excavation site. Write 200 words about the artifacts you discover. What do the artifacts tell you about the people who once lived at the site?

Say What?

Studying periods in ancient history can mean learning a lot of new vocabulary. Find five words in this book you've never heard before. Use a dictionary to find out what they mean. Then write the meanings in your own words and use each word in a new sentence.

Take a Stand

Archaeologists often disagree about what evidence says about people who lived long ago. Some archaeologists believe people arrived in North America by walking across the Bering Land Bridge. Others think people sailed there. What do you think the evidence tells us? Why do you think people care so much about the answers to these questions?

Another View

This book talks about different Paleo-Indian cultures. As you know, every source is different. Ask a librarian or another adult to help you find another source about these cultures. Write a short essay comparing and contrasting the new source's point of view with that of this book's author. What is the point of view of each author? How are they similar and how are they different?

GLOSSARY

archaeological
of or relating to the study of human history through artifacts or remains

artifact
an object made or left behind by a human

continent
one of Earth's main expanses of land

element
a chemical substance that can't be broken down any further than it already is

extinct
no longer living or existing

glacier
a mass of ice

migrate
to move from one place to another

obsidian
a kind of dark, hard, glassy volcanic rock

recede
to draw back or get smaller

terrain
the physical characteristics of land

transition
a change or shift from one thing to another

ONLINE RESOURCES

To learn more about the Paleo-Indian Period, visit our free resource websites below.

Visit **abdocorelibrary.com** or scan this QR code for free Common Core resources for teachers and students, including vetted activities, multimedia, and booklinks, for deeper subject comprehension.

Visit **abdobooklinks.com** or scan this QR code for free additional online weblinks for further learning. These links are routinely monitored and updated to provide the most current information available.

LEARN MORE

Hudak, Heather C. *The Archaic Period.* Abdo, 2025.

Millard, Anne. *The Ancient Worlds Atlas.* DK, 2023.

Milosavljevich, Stefan. *Tales of Ancient Worlds.* Neon Squid, 2022.

INDEX

About the Author

Emma Kaiser is a writer and educator based in western Minnesota. She has a master of fine arts degree in creative writing from the University of Minnesota, and her writing has appeared in several magazines and publications. She is the author of a number of other nonfiction books for students.